S0-ARK-698

Superpower

-Mercy

DOUGLASS BRANCH LIBRARY
Champaign Public Library
504 East Grove Street
Champaign, Illinois 61820-3239

Copyright © 2017 Mercy B Carruthers
Published by Mercy B Publications

All rights reserved. No part of this book may be
reproduced in any form without written consent of the
publisher, except brief quotes used in reviews.

I never believed in magic.

But, he had a **Superpower**.

$\mathcal{S}$uperpower

What is the first thought that comes to mind when the word is spoken?

My lips formed a curve, upward and wide. I couldn't help the smile in my eyes, either. I was no good at this topic –a total sucker for the "L" word. Shifting in my chair, I stared her in the face. I thought long and hard before my eyes shifted to the floor. I swung my legs over the coach before tucking them near my chin. Comfort was needed on the topic.

"Bliss. Pure bliss. When one utters the very intentional and meaningful four letter word, sparks fly. The skin on my face creases, and I, sometimes, gasp at the thought of penetration of the heart. I allow a giggle to evade my existence at the mention of it. The word itself brings my pulse to a racing height, expanding my senses —making me keen to every aspect of my surroundings. It's like, I am open at the mention of it -vulnerable, even. It's weird, but it's beautiful. It's thrilling to know that as strong of a woman that I am, this four-letter word has the power to shift my thoughts, mood, or even my day. The mere mention of the word has me questioning my strength. Seriously," I sighed, my eyes roaming over the neatly decorated room. The interior designer had skills. Nodding my head in satisfaction, I stared at the darkly tinted olive painted walls. The paint was still fresh. As I inhaled, the fumes invaded my nostrils. My shoulders slumped, and I began, again.

"Let's not even mention the afterthought. You know. The ache that soars through my chest, causing physical pain. As crazy as it is, it's never from current. The past afflictions that are associated with the word races to the forefront. Visuals of my slighted condition after fresh heartbreak consume my mental, and I'm reminded that although blissful, love can be horrific. Heinous."

He was right there. I could smell his dark skin, crisp and shimmering with the finest cocoa butter from the land. His fragrance of choice, Christian Dior Sauvage, caused me to choke on my own saliva. Hand to my chest, I tried to stop the impending pain that revisited with its master. A quick blink, and the single tear escaped my left eye, rolling down my cheek. I quickly swiped it, hoping that she didn't catch that.

Blinking, I willed him to disappear, and he did. *Just like always.* My smile returned with his exit. "So, yeah. The next question, please."

What is your definition of love, and how it feels?

"Mrs…" I paused. My memory failed me often. I had quickly forgotten her name. Squeezing my lids together, I chastised myself for the flaw.

"Weathers." She smiled, tugging at the name plate that sat on her chest, just above her padded bra and right breast.

"Weathers." I nodded. "How could you ask me to condense the meaning of a feeling so divine that man can't even stumble upon a common ground when it's noted? Let's think about what you're asking here. Love? Be defined?" I chuckled, my entire body quaking. It was a gesture of mine to hide the discomfort I felt in never really understanding the simple four letter word. For I had tried, but life had a way of proving me wrong every time. "I'd say that's taking things a bit far. I can't tell you what love is because every time you think you have it down pact, life happens and it makes you realize that just isn't it. I'm over ten years into the eventful quest to discover the true meaning. Do you have any insight?" I folded my arms, and sat back. "Please enlighten me."

With her pen to her chin, she stared at me through the thick lenses of her frames. The silence nearly smothered us both.

"See, Mrs. Weathers, this feeling… this wondrous feeling can't be defined… but expressed. Does that make sense?" I needed her input. I had no clue where this was going, but I had been in a space that I thought was love, and there was no way that I could define it. It was too, too much.

"Understood."

"Words could never equate to that rush… the spine tingling… nerve shaking… combustion of all things good and bad. The significance of love cannot be demarcated through vocab."

There he was, again. His smile was contagious, and appreciated. Everything about our connection was legendary. I could remember our first encounter. While it wasn't immediately that we sought out partnership, I knew that he'd be mine and vice versa. *Sometimes, you just know.* And there he stood, my evidence of love, yet there was no way I could sum him up in words.

Would you agree that it is a Superpower?

"Who thought of that?" My eyes searched the room as if someone else was present. "Because they're right. They're absolutely correct. How else could I explain the same feeling propelling me to heights far beyond my imagination… teaching me to soar? A feeling that summoned my soul and soothed it like a lullaby. Yet, the same feeling was nearly the blame for my demise. Well, it succeeded in killing my spirits, and then dragging me to the ground like a dog in the street."

My face contorted at the thought of the first time I should've let love become a pastime. I rolled my tongue over the top rack of teeth, and smirked.

Resting my head in my hand, I recalled the sound of my heart breaking, echoing in the distance.

"That shit is something serious. It should be considered a super drug as well. It's addictive in nature. Comforting. Alluring. It's one of those powers that everyone wants to possess. It's rich like wealth, and just like money… We'd do nearly anything to have it."

I nodded, and so did she.

"I never thought of it that way. Continue…" From the way my foot tapped the tiled floors, she could sense that I had more to say.

"It's so powerful that it makes you forget everything and anything that is not attached to it." I started to speak with my hands. They flew from the left to the right, bottom to the top. "It's like, you want to find it's entrance, go inside, and never come out. It's so amazing. I swear. When done right, this thing can be monstrous —in a great way. Inexorable. Unstoppable. Unrelenting. Just so damn whimsical."

I fell back onto the couch with a silly grin on my face. My cheeks burned, thinking about the days that we'd just lay. Nothing and on one else mattered in those moments but us. Calls went unanswered and texts were ignored. Until we were ready to emerge, we both remained submerged in the ambiance of one another's existence. Something as simple as the rhythm of his breathing calmed my entire being. *So surreal. Too good to be true.*

I shook my head from side to side, and turned my attention towards her. She was waiting… She had another question. I nodded, giving her the go.

With all that you've mentioned above, would you say that you've ever been in love? Ever felt that?

"I'd have to admit that *I* was in love." I was sure to emphasize the I. "Because, I was. Wholeheartedly."

My mind drew blanks as my face mirrored the pain I'd felt from the fragments it had left my heart in. I didn't need to wonder or figure out my standpoint on this question. There wasn't even a reason to drag it out. I was in love, deeply. It was the simplest question she had asked since we'd started.

Was it reciprocated?

"You know… Often in love, we are blind. We see what we want. We block out all things that don't fit in this little bubble that we place ourselves and our mates on. It's like, we construct this fantasy world, warding out impending forces against it. The signs are always bold, but we overlook them, selfishly wanting everything to be perfect and blemish-free. That's where we fuck up." I burst into laughter.

His eyes were so dark, staring me in the face. He, too, was hurting, because he knew that he couldn't offer me what I had, selflessly offered him. My chest rose and fell, seconds after one another. It pained me to breathe. My world was tumbling, and he wasn't even willing to pick it up or stop it —for he was the only one that had the power to.

My problem and solution. *My love*. Something within me died as we stood face to face, nose to nose. It would be two years before I could muster up the strength to sit in the spot that I sat today for the plethora of sessions that had come before this one.

Do you still hope that love will find you?

"As a hopeless romantic, it's the only option I have," I bit the corner of my thumb nail. The unevenness was driving me insane, or maybe I just needed a source of deflection. "Mrs. Weathers, when you smell the food, see it in front of you, touch the plate, and it burns your hand… Does it deter you from the meal placed in front of you?"

"No."

"You wait until it cools to the touch, right?"

"Correct."

"That's my sentiments. I've smelled it, and the thought of the taste alone makes me crave it. Although I was burned by that beautiful monster, I long to embrace it. I want love. I want it every day and all day. I want to wake to it, and bed to it as well. I'm simply in love with love. Until my dying day, whether I ever receive true love or not, I think that it will always be a desire of mine."

My eyes found the ceiling as I silently begged God to end my suffering. For this was me, a lover of all things, still mourning the loss of my love. I, desperately, wanted to move on to the more profound aspect of the four-letter word. I wanted the bliss and the beauty.

"But, only in God's timing." I smiled, finding her with my eyes.

"Mrs. Carruthers, I think that this concludes the day…" her voice trailed as I realized how much weight had been lifted from my shoulders.

After a year of visiting, today was the first that I felt like progress had been achieved. My heart danced inside of my chest as I thought of how much I'd needed the release that was just offered. On the upside, my heart was healing, and this visit had assisted me in realizing just that…

I Called Him Superman

Because at a point in time, I thought that he'd rescued my heart.

All of the nasty scars that had been left on the crimson covered vessel seemed to have been forced to depart

With each kiss…

Each touch…

Comfort rather than closure is what I was near

Silly of me…

To think that I…

Had found someone to erase those fears…

The fears that lingered with no plans to recant.

The fears that had kept me sheltered and not able to vent…

The fear that no man was heaven sent…

Truthfully, I was so hell bent on feeling something so good that it hurt...

Until I realized that it really did...

The neglect...

Denial...

And, back again, pain...

Your love had cut me deeper than what's that other guy's name...

My Superman

I'd trusted you with all that I had...

How could you just allow a good heart like mine to go bad...

Sour...

Smelly...

Dysfunctional...

Leaking...

And without use

Tell it, Superman, before me...

How many undeserving women did you do this to?

Were they perfect and willing to give you all of their love

Did they, too, get high off your potion like a junkie
strung out on drugs…
Did your engorged manhood swipe every nook and
cranny of their insides
Making them howl like wolves or belt out like
someone had died
Have you spoken with any of them lately…
Did they ever say the pain would subside…
Because it's been six long months…
And, for you, at night, I still cry…

Superman.

"If only you understood the nature of

my intent..."

Mercy

Something Between Us

Something between us

With each passing day I miss you more it seems,

Last night you were laying beside me,

But I woke up to realize it was only a dream,

As I slept you held me close,

I snuggled in your arms hoping you'd never let go,

With you everything just feels so right,

I want this thing between us to last for the rest of my life,

For us... I have hope and so much confidence,

In protection of our union, I want Jesus to be a fence,

Shielding us from problems that may come our way,

Because Lord knows with you is where I want to stay.

Sample of Something

"To Love and to Lose," by Mercy B

"Come here." Compton reached out and grabbed Ava, pulling her into his bosom.

"What?" she wined, an undeniable smile peeking out from behind her glossed lips.

"Don't what me." Compton laughed. "I missed you." He stated, honestly.

"I missed you, too." Ava replied.

A sinking feeling coursed through her veins as she was reminded of her reality. Fast paced, she was falling for Compton, without any ground near for safe landing. With them both being single, and Compton merely showing compassion, Ava resulted to the belief that she was falling alone. Even if that wasn't truthful, she had no such evidence that it wasn't.

"Kiss me, then."

It was moments like these that kept Ava from staying afloat. Effortlessly, Compton was penetrating her heart, and she wasn't too fond of it. However, the feeling that he gave her was like none other. He had gradually become her happy place. When she was without, she felt as if she was lacking. The undisputable thrill that soared through her limbs at just the thought of him kept her coming back for more. Compton was exciting, mainly because she never knew what she'd get from him. A wild card, he was.

If Only I Could Forget You Faster…

If only…

If only you weren't so near and dear to my heart…

If only the thought of you disappearing didn't tear me apart…

If only your forehead kisses and cuddles didn't mean so much…

If only it didn't pain at the thought of missing your touch…

If only you cared more or had a second thought before you did what you've done…

If only your logic would've reminded you that I was the one...

If only...
If only the stars would've twinkled that night...
If only I was the only to bring light to your life...
If only your love didn't become my addiction...
If only our static would've caused good friction...
If only you could've combated my predictions...
If only you would've proved me wrong...
If only I didn't have to listen to these stupid sad love songs...

If only you understood the nature of my intent...
If only you knew that my love was heaven sent...
If only you understood what companionship meant...
If only you didn't have me so fucking tense...
If only the urge to puke wasn't so strong...
If only you hadn't lead me on...
If only the world would stop denying our unification...

If only we were worth an attempt… a fight… a bit more patience…

If only you could've been perfect… in my eyes at lease…

If only you could've gotten in touch with your softer side, and trained the beast….

If only your engorged manhood didn't do me so good…

If only I could get over you… I would…

If only the thought of crying out your name didn't heighten my senses…

If only you wouldn't have ever showed me what it felt like to be fucked senseless…

If only this… and...

If only that…

If only I stop dwelling in the past and face the facts...

If only I could stop fantasizing about stating our vows in front of the pastor...

If only I could stop hearing us claim that "We Do," to the master…

If only…

If Only I Could Forget You Faster...

Superman

3:31

It's 3:31am,

I open my eyes and you're on my mind

I try to shake it,

But a smile like that is hard to find,

I try to break it,

But our connection is too divine,

I try to downplay it,

Like that dark handsome face ain't one of a kind,

It's 3:35am,

Now, I'm closing my eyes,

I'll try this again at a later time.

How could you just allow a good
heart like mine to go bad...
Sour...
Smelly...
Dysfunctional...
Leaking...
And without use... "

-Mercy

But Your Scars
They're Beautiful

As I pulled back the bandage, uncovering your imperfect and underexposed crevices, I also removed the thick layers of protection that guarded your most vital organ... the heart. The pain in your eyes, as we stared at one another, caused an inseparable mend between the two of us, for you were allowing me to undress your wound... territory that had gone undiscovered... and uncared for by any other.

The hissing in your tone nearly caused a spiraling coaster of sympathy, but I'd be nearly ashamed to evoke such emotion when there are millions more to explore. Rather than sympathizing with you, I galloped in glee FOR you.

For, I, too, have scars... uncovered and naked with truth. I revealed them just after I met you. With this simple revelation, I know that you've overcome and triumph would surely suit well on your resume of choice. Now that the barricade is unrooted, here comes my voice...

"But your scars, they're so beautiful."

The salty mixture that cascaded from my eyes fell to the surface -cleansing your most beautiful flaw. With your free hand, you wipe away the tears that your nudeness has caused. That's just the way it works. You give me the glory, and then snatch away the perks. You're not only the problem, but you're the solution, too. Just when I want to run far away, I run to you.

Right after your mess, you beg of me to allow you to clean it up. That's the reason we're in this position, now... You looking down, and I'm looking up.

I asked if you could reveal to me the problem that urges you to do what you do... You know that thing where the pain that you cause is so unbearable that I can barely move...

"What's hurting you?" I sounded like a love-sick fool... And here I am, now, staring back at your naked truths...

One Million Reasons

You deep dove into my life...

Made everything alright...

Stripped me of my past,

But for you I was willing to make the sacrifice...

Humbled my heart...

Took control of my soul...

Gave me something to hold on to...

And I'll never let go...

But as your good energy transferred,

Becoming another good deed of yours to bestow...

Something shifted...

Something broke...

Like the smile that was bright as the morning sun...

Why the sadness Chosen One?

Why the crease in your neatly lined forehead...

Why the emotional outbursts...

Why the belief of what he or she said?

Hadn't I seen your victorious nature.

I wouldn't know of the brilliance you were called to be...

But this is you... and this is me...

You brought me back from hanging on a limb...

You were never like that...

No comparison to them...

Your ability was strong...

Wavering...

Had a enough fucking courage to sway a nation...

Now, I'm looking at you... broken and done...

Come back to me smile... bright like the morning sun...

The roles have been reversed...

My time has come...

It's my turn to uplift you...

Though I don't have much, maybe your line will help some...

Reverse physiology... huh?

Like you said. "I don't need a million reasons to love you. you gave me one..."

When was...

When was the last time?

You received a delivered notice from the "Good Morning" text you sent me…

You thought of my contagious smile and found yourself smiling

You pressed send for the last time before bed to that "Goodnight" text I smiled from upon receipt even while half asleep

You caught me by surprise with a FaceTime date prompting me to get up from my nap and rid of my head wrap

You genuinely craved my presence

You stopped and thought "I wonder what she's doing"

You expressed that you missed me because you know
in your heart that our distance kills me softly every
day in every way

You just told me you loved me knowing you would
cause a sea of butterflies in my tummy and a loud
thud of my heart

Huh, when was the last time?

Discovery

Seemingly, when she discovered her worth, no amount of lies could bring her back. No amount of pacifying could soothe her soul. No amount of words could talk her into staying. No amount of tears could move her. No amount of pleading could make her reconsider. No amount of history could keep her. No amount of maturity could change her opinion.

And just like the sun on a stormy night, her presence was yearned. Her absence plagued the one she'd chosen... The lesser. And in that moment, he, too, discovered just how much she was worth.

Ever been **fucked**,

mentally?

He Fucked Me

It's been said that mental sex was the best. I would've never backed the myth had I not put it to the test.

Back in Feb 2013, I met a man. I'm nearly ashamed to tell of how I shed my belongings, stripping for him... Baring it all... Just so he could fuck me. And he did... He fucked me. He fucked me, mentally.

I thought that it would be one of those "hit it and quit it" type deals. I'll even admit that I was the first to initiate the fucking, of my mental that is. I challenged everything that he stood against. See, I was from out of town, and you know how that story usually goes. "One night only, I'm from out of town."

The famous lyrics of Yo Gotti was probably the motive behind his tactics. Silly of him. Even after our "physical" departure, I felt a slight connection. With the small inkling, I dared him to do something that hadn't been done... stimulate my mind. Boy, you'd better be careful what you ask for.

Mental stimulation was the greatest gift he could've ever given me. After our initial encounter, when the smoke had cleared, my mental arousal was so prominent that I could think of nothing more than taking things to the next level. The absence of the physical (eyes, arms, legs, fingers, toes, hands, and more) was furthest from mind.

Besides, not even his hardened member could outdo the mental penetration of my mind, body, and soul. The stroking of my ego and most sensual cells was better than anything I've ever felt.

With an untouched box, I fell for him... Not physically... But mentally. Back and forth... In and out... My word did this man feel so good to me. He filled me up with his massiveness over and over.

Before the thrill had even ended. I knew I'd be coming back... again... And again.

He wasn't a quick pumper, either. He really took his time. Grinding, he was sure to put a constant smile on my face. Each time I felt myself getting low... heavy with burdens, his sweet nothings that were being whispered into my ear soothed all -as he continued to pound away. I could barely move a muscle as I succumbed to his vicious strokes. He really knew his way around. I was smitten at his reassuring ways.

Holding me in place, he prepared to take me on a wave. Higher and higher. I climbed... Finally reaching the ultimate climax. Shooting his best shot, his complexity took control. That was just fine... because at the point of mental relaxation. I could barely think straight.

In fact. I'd much rather him think for me -at this point. Tangled and twisted. I basked in the ambience... slightly saddened at the realization that some day I'd have to come down from where I'd been placed. And just as I thought... I came tumbling down like that girl Jill right after Jack.

But... Damn...

He fucked me so good that I can still feel him inside of me. *It's been days since we last spoke, but I can still feel him... fucking me... mentally.*

Sample of Something

The gloom covered my lids as I elongated my neck in anticipation of, yet, another deep thrust. Sonnie's erection broke through my walls with little to no resistance as he transferred the feelings of guilt from his being to mine. It had been a full month since our flesh had united.

With the revelation of his infidelity, I'd concluded our 5-year relationship with the hopes of never returning to the position that we were currently in - back arched, ass in the air. Completely throwing all caution through my bedroom window, I had allowed this man back into my bed and within my sheets.

Sympathy consumed me as I felt wetness seeping down my spine. Our separation had cause an irreparable rift that we both knew could never be mended. Partially numb to the pain, I felt Sonnie reach for me, pulling me upward as he continued to make love to me -mind, body, and soul. Hands around me neck, chin tucked at my shoulder. Sonnie went to mumble in my ear, but nothing came to. Groans and moans, from both parties, were the only vocal expression constructed.

Exercising more forceful withdrawals and insertions, Sonnie allowed his actions to speak for him. "I'm sorry," was well within each stroke. Back and forward. In and out. He rocked my body like a newborn baby cradled in it's mother's arms fresh from birth.

Short after our climaxes, Sonnie prepared himself to leave. I was conflicted in the worst way as I watched him buckle his Gucci jeans -ones that I'd splurged on for his 28th birthday.

The anxiety that swelled in my chest was to be mistaken for nothing other than the result of a dark cloud that had been circling around my head for the past week. It was the very reason I had invited Sonnie over to be sure that all was well with him. As of lately, death had been knocking at my door, and I was afraid that someone near me would be the one to answer. The life that Sonnie lived placed his name at the head of my prayer list.

Although my limbs were fragile, I attempted to lift myself from the bed.

"Don't worry. I'll lock up." He lifted his hand, putting a halt to my miserable attempt at standing.

Seconds later, he was out of the bedroom that we'd once shared. As I listened to him paddle down the hall, my breathing became shallow the second he footsteps became faint.

"Maybe he's coming back…" I thought to myself.

I was proved wrong as I heard the creeping of the bedroom door just a few feet away from mine. Again, I reminded myself that I needed to put a bit of oil on the hinges of Sonja's pink princess themed door.

I listened, in silence, as Sonnie made a mess of my daughter's face. I didn't have to be present to know that the kiss noises meant that he was showing her love in it's highest regards. That was his world. When it came to our baby girl, the fiends, the corners, the traps, or the shipments didn't matter. As one would say, home was where his heart was.

As fast as my heart had settled, the pace of its beating went into overdrive as he pulled the squeaky door back closed. Next, he descended the steps, driving me insane each time his feet tapped the wooden surface.

"Just tell him to stay the night…" I was at war with my very own mind, battling the thought of looking weak or standing my ground.

As his feet touched the 12th step, I jumped from the bed. My strength had come back, immediately. I had counted down, and knew this was my final chance. Throwing my silk robe over my slim frame, I, then, slipped my feet into a pair of slippers as well.

Rushing down the stairs, I witnessed Sonnie pulling the front door open. I didn't utter a word, but picked up the pace. My feet were shuffling a mile a minute to get to him, and reached the doorway just as he turned to shut it behind him.

"Please, just st…" my words were cut prematurely.

The sound of a single gunshot paralyzed me, momentarily. My thoughts had retracted, and my mind became void of the very awareness of my own existence.

I didn't regain consciousness until I felt brain matter spew onto my face. Eyes wide as saucers, I tried to mentally process what was being orchestrated in front of me. The weight of Sonnie's body dropped to the ground like a sack of charcoal, taking mine with it.

"Sonnie." My voice was barely audible as I looked down at his distorted features. His smooth cocoa skin had been pulled backwards, exposing the mind that I loved with every ounce of me.

Like a howling wolf, I cried out. "LORD! NO! NO!" My vocal box burned as his crimson colored blood poured onto my silk robe, "PLEASE. NO! SOMEBODY HELP!"

My hands shook, dramatically, contemplating on getting help or staying put. Emotionally incompetent, I stared back at our front door. Death had knocked, and my Sonnie had answered.

Dream Girl

I want to be a touchy subject for him, his weakness, that one soft spot, the one thing he handles with care, his happy place, his fragile being, his undeniable love bug ...

#letagirldreambeforebedsometime

Something Happened Somewhere

Is it your purpose to hurt me?

Stumble upon my heart...

Pick it up...

Then desert me...

Is my pain the cause of your erection...

Head spinning...

Mind saying no...

Heart headed in the other direction...

Let's be honest, there's just something about this
connection...

Please, allow me a second to vent...

See because the day that we met I thought we were
meant...

Enamored by your charm,

I've been fucked up ever since...

Chest pounding...

Body tense...

I must admit that it hasn't always been like this

In the beginning, I was on the fence...

But as time would have it, love settled my suspense...

Like the air that we breathe, nearly impossible to

condense...

Big. Wide. Unattainable in a sense...

I just want to go back to where our thing

commenced...

Maybe my words could've been more firm that day...

Maybe I should've left you the first time it happened

to let you know that I didn't play...

Maybe my hair was a bit too pretty...

Maybe my laugh was a bit too giddy...

Maybe my demeanor was a little too laxed...

Help me out here....

I'm just trying to think back...

Way way back to where this went wrong...

Was it the first day that I called and you didn't answer your phone...

Was it before or after the first time we made love...

Was it before the fussing back and forward...

I'm running out of thoughts like we've run out of time...

I guess I'll just have lay the questions on the line...

You know... For the sake of my sanity and peace of mind...

I'm convinced that this one wasn't ours...

Maybe I'll see you next lifetime...

Sample of Something

"Ain't Nothing Wrong with Missing Somebody"
-A short by Mercy B

"I don't wanna open my eyes... You give me life... You ease my mind... Like a lulla-lullaby." -Tink

As a hopeless romantic, my mind often trails to the topic of love (good or bad). Even in my novels, they're filled with profound... uncanny... heart shattering... earth-quaking... misunderstood... magical... heart warming... Pure... Deep... Love.

I'm just in love with love.

As I dig, and get personal, I must admit that I haven't had the best luck with relationships or in love. Even with that in mind, I realize that one day God will send some worthy man on a journey to find me. When he is upon me, I'll know. With everything that I've got, I'm going to love him into a frenzy. Together, we will embark on something unique, genuine, and uncompromising.

But until that day... I'm missing somebody... Well, not them... Their presence.

I'm not certain if it's the vision I had that they completely ruined that has me upset, or the way things played out. I wouldn't even be surprised if it's the nights like this that I get frustrated thinking about the greatness we could've created, as one, that gets me riled up.

Perhaps the fact that they seem to be enjoying life as my entire world has stopped that grinds my gears. I don't know what it is, or maybe it's everything... Maybe it's nothing.

Whatever the case is, none of the above has changed two certainties that I struggle with. 1) I still love 'em. 2) I miss 'em... Well, not them, but their presence.

There's only seven days in a week, and five in a work week. Each of those days, I find myself wanting to reach out. But not for him, just his voice. Quiet nights, laying alone in my bed, feeling the space just left of me... I wish the emptiness was replace with his body... Not him... Just his body.

There's been a few days that I've felt the weight of the world, and if only I could've gotten a forehead kiss from him... Not him... Just his kisses. They've always been the sweetest.

Drastic decisions that involve too much confusion, thinking, or attention, I wish to borrow his thoughts... Not him... Just his thoughts. Scrolling through my messages, I often want to replace nearly half of the feed with his name... Not him... Just his name.

As bizarre as this may sound, it's reality for the most of us. We want everything that they have to offer, but not them. We often miss the warmth of their being, invading our personal space. We miss the corny jokes, and the small reasons they give us to smile.

We miss how calm our world was before the storm. We miss the relief, comfort, and confidence we felt before it all went south. If we could just... capture their presence. It would be a beautiful sight, huh?

"La La La La... La La La La... You ease my mind like lullaby,"

"And just like the sun on a stormy night, her presence was yearned. Her absence plagued the one she'd chosen... The lesser. And in that moment, he, too, discovered just how much she was worth."

Mercy

"Discovery"

Thinking of My Thoughts

My thoughts are aligned with your existence

My heart admired your persistence

With you, there was never any resistance,

Willing... Able... to give you what you were missing.

Mentally and emotionally...

Mind blowing when speaking of the physic

Because, I desired to explore you like nature...

Watch out for you like a good neighbor

Be the one to call when you needed a favor..

Fuck you good... Suck you better...

Not talking about now... That was later...

Yeah... later...

Much like a waiter...

I could've waited...

Hand and foot...

But it seems as if your adoration has dissipated...

I'm reaching out... Stepping out... with no one to save me...

Eyes flickering... Heart racing...

Even in your disappearing act I need to tell you that this has been amazing...

My Chest Hurts

BriAnn Danae - Author

What is your definition of love?

I chuckled. Deep down, I knew that would be her first question so I was prepared. Squaring my shoulders straight ahead, I gave her a soft smile. "One time I googled what love meant. You know, the generic version that can be searched on the web, defined by an anonymous person that no one is ever going to meet."

She didn't chuckle at my humor, but did give me a head nod to continue. Going through my rolodex, I recalled the memory of when I first expressed I loved someone. Loved *him* rather. I was in high school. He was my first, everything. That thought made me roll my eyes.

"I'd define love as a deep feeling for someone or something. That um," I stopped and licked my lips. "That connection of knowing whatever they do or say, can affect your wellbeing as they see fit. I mean, if you let them of course. If you let love affect your wellbeing."

And that it did. On many occasions, I'd find myself smiling for no reason. Anticipating the next time I'd see his face, hear his voice, inhale his scent. I'd lose track of time from simply daydreaming about us. About the possibilities of what love, or the thought of had in store for us.

Have you ever been in love & how was that feeling?

My throat became clogged. Shit! That question brought upon déjà vu immediately. Once again, I was taken down memory lane. I'd proudly proclaimed that I loved two men in my life, but I didn't want to remember how it felt.

Thinking back to how I lost myself in them, not with them. Why did I even agree to this interview? Was love really that complicated to figure out?

"I don't think, well, perhaps I was almost there," I said, bringing my index finger and thumb close together in a pinch. "Have I verbally said I'm in love with you? No. Did I feel like I was? Definitely. It's a scary feeling," I chuckled, to hide the mask of hurt that tried breaking free across my face.

Eyes wandering to the high-rise buildings through the window, I inhaled a deep breath. "Are you afraid of heights?" She shook her head no.

"That's how it felt. One minute you're high on life, and love, in the sky where nothing or no one can reach you. No one seemed to even be allowed to breathe the same air that I was in, because I didn't want to share that feeling with anyone. Selfish, right? But, that's how I felt. I was so high off something I knew could damn well damage me had I been pushed from that high place. Kill me even."

I felt my answer was good enough, but I was still in my head. Goosebumps covered my arms, inched down my spine, and my throat dried thinking of the way *he* loved me and how… how it was so good at one point. I never wanted our phone calls to end. His laugh when I said something corny was one I'd never forget.

How he spoke so loudly whenever he was joking around or pissed off, but low and luxurious when we were good. The sound of his voice early in the morning, when he rolled over and asked how I slept, had me biting my lip and squeezing my eyelids tight. Because God knows we had been up all night exploring one another's body how lovers do. I slept peacefully those nights.

And then, there were nights when I choked back tears because he hadn't reached out to me in days. I contemplated on pulling up to his crib, or wherever he was supposed to be at and showing my ass. But I knew that would get me nowhere. Us, nowhere. He was no longer attentive to the mental part of me, nor the physical. He didn't know that my mind was so gone, that my body followed without orders.

That, he could ask something of me and I'd oblige willing because… shit, love. It was no big deal for him to see me out months later, whisper in my ear how he missed me, and asked me to link up before the club let out.

Oh, but see that's where those feelings came into play. I still loved him, you see. Regardless of him not responding to my semi lengthy texts until hours later once I was over it. Or the fact that he'd be on social media "expressing" himself to meaningless mufuckas who didn't even know his middle name. He didn't have one. We'd still have sex. Makeup sex in a sense, but there was no getting back together. Clearly.

The mornings after were always awkward. Especially when we hugged. We each squeezed a little tighter, and I never wanted to let go because we "felt" right. And on my ride home, I'd get those feelings in check because I knew it would be a while before I would be in his presence again. Though my mind said it would be okay... it's just sex... my heart couldn't take it.

"Just imagine being without something you've never gone without, eh? Not willingly of course. Air for instance. Being in love or the thought of it, made me feel like I couldn't breathe. And damn sure not on my own."

Did you think it was real?

"More authentic than those bundles in your head." We laughed together at that one. "Seriously, though. I knew it was real once I was completely over him, and then he began to act how I did when he'd go missing on me. Distance does things to the heart. Some good, and some so bad it's hard to speak about it."

She nodded her head, as I stared off into space once again. My stomach felt tight and I began questioning myself about all those years I announced my love for him, and how it was reciprocated every time except for the last few times. His answer would be "I know you do, man." As if, me loving him was so wrong. Could he blame me?

Surely not when I had become a permanent fixture in his life for so long. Not just to him, but his family and friends as well. Though, their opinions of what we had going on didn't matter. Even when we'd both say on different occasion that we couldn't keep doing this… whatever *this* was. I now know this meant hurting each other. Or maybe it meant stringing each other along.

Whatever the case, what we had was toxic. Nothing how I projected love to be nor feel. I didn't want to feel sick, and crying because I couldn't come to sorts with the way my heart and mind should react to certain things. I no longer wanted to be that girl not telling her friends how bad of a day I had all because a man, whom they knew I loved, no longer loved me.

Because, let's be honest… that's what it was. When someone stops making you feel a certain way, and your wellbeing can function without them, it's safe to say that whatever we had was a wrap. I could breathe again. And stand on that tall building in the sky and share my air with someone else and gladly say that love had treated me fairly. It was the person I *loved*, that wasn't prepared for what I had to give.

Contributed by BriAnn Danae

Used to it

So used to the pain you bring...

Then there's the finer things...

Apologies, roses, cards, and shiny rings...

It's all redundant...

So routine...

Good as...

I'm as good as I'm going to get at my worst...

Broken and disgusted...

You know, because you noted it first...

You mentioned the real me...

The no makeup, sweats baggy... the chill me...

Because in those moments I'm less guarded and even without your fingers you can feel me...

I just never grasped the concept of it being the lesser you'd rather see...

But then you mentioned God and how his creations aren't to be tampered...

Only what he created them to be...

Rather that's hype, buck, happy, and upbeat...

Or weary, afraid, and overcome with defeat...

And simply at the notion my weary eyes grow with big and round...

For I'm still amazed at your ability to turn my
darkened days upside down...
"It requires less muscles to smile than frown."
Ha! That's the shit that I have to look forward to...
Simple statements in rebuttals to help me become a
better reflection of you...

So mighty... macho... bold... and true...
If I had to reimburse for all that you do,
Forever indebted...
My heart, mind, and body would belong to you...
From your little gift & curse...
I love you for understand that I'm my best at my
worst...

Black Man, I Love You

Dear Black Man, I Love You

For now, I want to remind my black man just how much he is loved and appreciated. In a world where they're being murdered and pursued as the big bad wolves, we must continue to pour good faith into our black men. No one is gong to do it for us. Women, be the Queen. When a simple encounter with the police can be the moment he takes his last of breaths, and be sent to the glory, we must lift him up while he's still on borrowed time. If you have a black man, know a black man, or will soon encounter one, here's to him.

Dear Black Man,

I love you. I love you like the bees love honey, and the banks love money. I know that line was corny, but I had to start with something funny. After all that's happening, now, I wanted to give you a reason to smile before I commanded your time for a little while.

On a more serious note, I love you for your rich chocolate stature, and line of unfiltered heritage. Even if you're worthless to others, you mean the world to me. Whether it's the wrinkles within your aging skin or the dimming of your dark eyes, they tell a complete story of strife, lack of acceptance, cruelty, pain, injustice, anger, and worry... For you don't know what your tomorrow holds. Yet, and still, you're beautiful, black man.

Black man, you owe no apology for your broad features and manly curves. Your shell is so true to your culture, and it's awe-striking. You're built like a precious fixture in my grandmother's living room... You're made so wonderfully. My God, he was showing out when he created you. I brag... I'll admit that I brag about you all of the time. Your dark hair, eyes, large lips, round nose, and facial hairs. Everything is placed so perfectly. I just love you, black man.

Black man, your strength is commendable. Each time you're knocked down, you get back up. You remind me of one of those Tom and Jerry episodes, determination being your strong suit. Those millions of times when I couldn't give 100% of what God had given, you simply poured more of your goodness into my cup. That's why I love black man. Even with calloused hands, strong facial features, and arms claimed by muscle... You're the gentle giant that no one wants to learn to understand, but I do, black man.

Black man, I'm gushing over you. Don't you see that? While everyone is gunning you down, I'm appalled at your will to place your armor on and go to war each day. I'm not just meaning physically. I'm talking mentally, emotionally, and spiritually. It's amazing how you fight those mental battles while smiling and

carrying on about your day. You never let your
emotions get the best of you while you're heading the
dinner table and bowing to pray... God, it must be so
difficult to keep your faith... When your brothers are
being killed everyday... But black man, if you walked
out of our house just after kissing the children, and
was gunned down today, know that we love you...
And your worries as a black man have been taken
away.

But wait...
Wait...

Black man, I'm raising your son. The harsh realities
of his future keeps me up at night. Black man, how do
I overcome the fact that my baby boy will be slighted
simply by the color of his skin. You have the answers
that I so desperately seek. Next time, can we talk
about this before you lay down to sleep? Because, as
his parent, I want the world to love him just as I do,
much like your mother loved you. Black man, forgive
me for flipping the strip, but the concern arose as I

thought of all that's unsure. I'll rest my case until you're home from work. I'm not you, black man. I can never be. So, please enlighten me on the well-being of our seed.

I had a moment of uncertainty...
My apology...
Back to you...

Black man, you're the definition of excellence. Everything about you is worth a hoot and a holler. The bells and the whistles. The fun and the fancy. From your head to your toe, you should be clothed in the finest garments, bathed with pure glitter and silk, acknowledge when your presence is upon others, celebrated in a major way, gather the harps to sing, and rightfully be crowned King.

It's my duty as your Queen, to open up... And remind you that you are beautiful. You are bold. Your are strong. You are important. You are black... You are a black man... You are a BELOVED black man.

Sincerely,

Your Black Queen.

Your dark skin, radiant

like the moon...

Mercy

You Feel so Good

The thudding in my chest is so intentional

It's like you fuck my visual

Then move on to my mental

This fingering you're reigning on my intellectual

Got me steaming hot... mad cause I let you

Even just being around... here with you

Got you massaging my spiritual

My mind is saying no,

I could only wish that my body would...

It's been damn near two weeks and them long strokes

still feel so fucking good...

Sample of Something

"To Love and to Lose" by Mercy B

"I just can't, anymore." Saydee gently shook her head as the salt-filled droplets tumbled down her swollen cheeks. For the past hour she'd been crunched in a corner, the same place that Leon had left her. After an atrocious hour of horror, Saydee was just thankful to still have breath in her lungs. The constant pain that struck every time she inhaled reminded her of the many jabs that Leon had strategically landed at her midsection.

Blood seeped from the crotch area of Saydee's distressed denim as she cried to herself. Too afraid to move, she prayed that Leon left soon. With the pain that she was feeling, it was understood that she'd be a while getting up. Saydee didn't want to run the risk of Leon catching her trying to get up, and have him to force her back down to the floor.

Squeezing her eye lids together, tightly, Saydee thought about how foolish she must've sounded for being so cowardly, but it really wasn't the case. Love had driven her to this point. True love, as she used to call it. Had anyone told her three years ago that the start of her relationship with Leon would lead to destruction, she would've told them to go to hell –just before peeling off in one of her dearest Leon's foreign whips.

The start of their relationship was peachy, as all. Now, three years into their union, Saydee wasn't even allowed out of the house without the invisible leash that Leon had wrapped around her neck. Looking back, she tried to remember at what point had things gotten so bad between the two. With her mind trained on the past, she guessed that their turning point was probably the time when Leon found a co-worker's number inside of her phone and shoved her into the kitchen counter –causing a bruise on her back. Shamefully, Saydee quickly remembered that it had started way before that. As early as the first year, she recollected the way that Leon would squeeze her wrist or arm while trying to get his point across.

It was a small gesture, but she should've recognized the warning signs. They were always there. His need to know her every move, and the tampers he'd throw if he didn't. Even the amount of cellphone data usage was monitored by his craziness. Saydee was forbidden to do anything without his consent or knowledge. Often, she wondered if wiping her ass after a shit was even okay.

Shaking her thoughts, Saydee slowly turned her body towards the corner of the wall that she was slouched on and strained her eyes to see better. Peering into the bedroom of the enormous mansion that she called home, Saydee watched as Leon dressed. It was such a shame that a man so handsome could be so vicious. As charming as he was, he was lethal.

For the third time, Saydee had found herself pregnant and all alone. Her pregnancy resulted in her very last beating. Leon was completely against children. Yet, he couldn't find the decency to stop pumping them into her. An abortion clinic wasn't even an option due to his home remedy –beating the baby out of her. Granted, Saydee didn't want any children by Leon; however, she hated him for killing her unborn children.

Two minutes passed before Saydee watched Leon place his pistol in his waistband before pulling his shirt over the black handle. Throwing on his Kentucky State fitted cap, he grabbed his cell and keys before heading for the bedroom door. Quickly placing her back against the wall, again, Saydee placed her head into her lap.

Distance

I'd rather adore you from a distance. Close range, that's when shit gets different. Lines get twisted. Forevers get iffy.

Simple Satisfactions

My lids stretched to meet the morning sun. I was beyond exhausted from traveling just the day before. The pounding of my head reminded me of my night out with the bottle, causing a smile to erupt from the corners of my eyes to the corners of my mouth. Sighing, I reached over and logged into my twitter account.

Telephone numbers... Bank account numbers... Easily confused on my end. Bada-bing Bada-boom. (shrugging emoji)

As I slept, dollars were flying across my forehead. Had I been a victim of normalcy, then it may have been sheep. However, the way that my world had been predesigned, I had no time to count anything but. My thoughts aligned with my father, RahMeek Jones. I could remember all the Valentine's that lead up to my 20th birthday being conspired by him. I wondered, as I matured, why my father went all the way out for me on the day that was designated for your significant other, but I later discovered his truth. He was preparing me, and showing me that I deserved nothing but the best of everything.

My father was laying the foundation, and he'd laid a solid one. Bracing myself, I thanked God for another day and prepared to meet my lover for a late breakfast. The purpose of my travels was to show my support at his game the following day. Fabian, my boyfriend of a year, had promised to make this day as special as the ones before it, so I was trusting him on this.

Top of the morning. Let's see how well my Valentine thought out the day. I tweeted.

Sitting up, I tossed my cell to the side and stretched my arms above my head. They came down with a thud, smacking my legs under the cover. I felt a soft, silky substance under the length of my arm, causing me to redirect my eyes.

"Get out of here!" I smiled, holding my hand over my mouth.

There were red roses sprawled across the bed, covering the fresh, clean, white linen. My cheeks burned as I began to wonder how Fabian had been able to sneak this pass me. I must've really been gone the night before. Thinking back, I figured this was all his plan. He'd been sure to have room service supply my favorite wine for my landing.

My eyes partied around the spread, landing on a breakfast tray with the bold Tiffany & Co. box sitting in the center of white chocolate covered strawberries. "Wait. White chocolate?" I giggled, completely out of my element.

So used to my father showering me, this almost seemed unreal. Of course, I was accustomed to the gadgets, but the producer of them made all the difference. From my father, the best was to be expected. However, this was a human with no actual obligations to me.

Reaching over, I grabbed the pretty blue box, and was stunned at the diamond bracelet that gazed into my eyes. My face became flushed, and the lump in my throat thickened. Fabian was a dream, and I was happy to have him as my reality. Turning backwards in bed, I searched for his darling smile, but he was nowhere in sight.

I didn't bother putting the bracelet on, because I wanted him to do the honors. Reaching over, I grabbed the note that was gathered by the tray. My fingers were moving a mile a minute as I shared the start of my day with my twitter feed. My face dropped when I read the scribbling on the card.

There's more bling to come. Leave your cell where it's at. No phone zone. –Fab

Blushing, I ended my Twitter story, and tried to contain my nerves. I had just awakened, and my day had already been made. *What else does this man have in store for me,* I questioned myself.

Sleeping with clothing caused a rift in my anxiety, so I slept with as less as possible. Last night was capped off in the nude, which lead me to pulling the covers from my bare skin. Walking into the bathroom, I decided to handle my hygiene before getting Fabian on the line. I needed him in my presence, like yesterday.

Before I could step into the bathroom, fully, I was halted by the writing across the Jack and Jill style vanity mirror.

"HURRY!" I spoke, reading the single word that had been printed in red lipstick.

Pausing, tracing my makeup bag, hoping that Fabian wasn't crazy enough to fuck with my collection of lipsticks. Then, it hit me that I didn't carry a red lippie. The color made me look a few years ahead of my time, so I resisted it. I stuck to nudes and shades close to it.

Proceeding, I stepped into the bathroom as if I was on a mission. Laughter erupted from my lungs as I realized what I was about to do. Instead of brushing my teeth, I squeezed a decent amount of toothpaste onto my index finger and stuck it in my mouth. For ten seconds, I twirled it inside, and then rinsed.

Shrugging, I dried my hands and made my way back into the bedroom. The cool breeze from the air conditioner made chill bumps rise on my skin, and my nipples harden. I stalked back into the room, and stumbled backwards in surprise.

"Reign." Fabian looked up at me with a worried smile. "I…"

Finally gaining my composure, I began fanning my face. The once cold room had become torched. The flames were eating away at my toes, and moving upward towards my legs. This was not happening to me. Fabian was not on his knees, and I was not witnessing a small square box inside of his hand.

With his light brown skin and one dimple on display, my heart swelled. I had never admired his pretty white teeth so openly, but I couldn't help the fact that they were on full display. Fabian's muscles bulged from his shirt, stirring my emotions even more. Everything seemed so perfect, and there he was. He was still on one knee.

"Get up… Get up…" they were the only words that would come to as I wiped my tears with the back of my hand. "Baby, get up." I cried, chest caving and rising –caving and rising.

"Reign Baylee Jones," his disobeyed. "I love you with everything in me. I know it's only been a year, but it doesn't take a lifetime to know when you've found the one. You're it for me. I feel it in my soul, hear it in your voice, see it in your eyes, and witness it every time you smile. You make me whole, baby girl. There's nothing on God's green earth that I wouldn't do for you. I want to continue making memories, but with you as my other half. Will you do me the honor of being my wife?"

Hot and Cold

I swear it's like hunting for eggs with you, not knowing what you'll get. Or even deciding what to wear in the spring the night before not knowing that the weather may bring... Oh yeah right, or even tasting a new dish for the very first time not knowing if you'll fall in love or absolutely hate it. Or even going to a new hair dresser, unsure if you guys will be a good fit. Hot and cold.

In that moment, there was

a slight delegation...

I took on your world and

you returned the favor.

Mercy

"Meeting Was Magic"

Rearranging Stars

For you, I'd rearrange stars...

Boil over like hot lava emitting from the volcanoes of Mars...

I wouldn't mind sharing with you... for we'd have two moons...

Let's forget the Sun, and in darkness become consumed...

165 years to revolve... Neptune...

For you, I'd rearrange stars...

Run laps around Saturn's rings,

Cause you're some type of magic...

Bada boom... bada bing...

For you, I'd rearrange stars...

Gently kiss your oversized heart...

If I had to use my prediction...

Baby Jupiter can't be as large...

Hey... I'm no expert... Astrologist, I'm not...

But chemistry keeps assuring me of this thing we've got...

For you, I'd rearrange stars...

Cuff you some bling...

Uranus couldn't mind...

There's 8 more rings...

Take you down to Pluto and make your body sing...

Legs quiver... quake... amongst other things...

Your adventurous eyes...

Brown in color as the Venus skies...

This shit we have is deeper than soul ties...

Cause when we unite...

The universe shifts... Things collide...

The surface heats...

Burning my soul like Mercury.

Come 'er boo...

I'm bringing you back to Earth with me...

Where did you go Missing?

Somewhere.

I'm not sure at what point or place that you stumbled into my grace... But it feels like you've been here before... Not meaning from the recent encounter the other day. You've had to have been here, it's the only reason to explain this friction... it's the only way to sum up acquiring such a thing that you had no clue you'd been missing.

Maybe it's true that it's two lifetimes that we live to see... Because in our prior one, I was apart of you... and you were a part of me.

So, forget the formal... But it's truly nice to meet you, again. If this shit all ended today, I pray that we're given another lifetime, or maybe even ten,

if it means that in each one I'd still meet you, friend.

Meeting Was Magic

Fuck it, I'll call you Tsunami for this,

The way you that you sauntered into my site...

Like a beautiful bliss..

Disruptive & uplifting by nature,

I'm slick upset at how the world portrays you,

Deadly, dangerous, a hazard to health,

"Get up... High... On top of something... Protect
yourself,"

Those are the procedures... the false information.

Yet, I stood there and embraced you, despite the
allegations.

In that moment, there was a slight delegation...

I took on your world and you returned the favor.

Right in front of me, you stood, dark like the night...

handsome as the rising of the sun...

Unlike the rest of them, I stood 10 toes down...

I didn't buckle... I didn't run...

And what a gorgeous structure that stood in front of me...

A fresh & clean start is all you seek...

No wonder you were created from a body of water that runs so deep...

Tsunami, true to character...

As a wave... thoughts of your essence rocked me to sleep....

Giving In

As much as I would've loved to fight the urge to reach out tonight, giving in was easier. Mainly because giving in allowed me another chance to communicate with you -even if only once. Giving it allowed me to embrace the desires I've been neglecting every night that I've wanted to just say hello. Giving in eased my mind. Giving in gave way to all those endless possibilities that I once saw for us. So now that I've given in, hello ❤.

Superpower

Thank You

BriAnn Danae: Thanks for the contribution to this project. I'm happy that you were able to express yourself, even for a second. Sometimes we need a little outlet. Glad that I could be a fix, somehow.

Author of, "My Chest Hurts."
www.BriAnnDanae.net

Superman: We've all had him before. Whether he's laying next to you now or you wish to never see his handsome face again, at some point your heart was his. Maybe it still is.

They say that once you love a man, you'll love him forever. I'm certain that whoever made the revelation is a smart being.

For one will love *Superman* until the world blows. Some things you can't get around, under, or over. In distance or near, your heart there and his heart here *—reading this endnote.*

MERCY B CARRUTHERS

Let's Connect

Social Media

You can find me on all social platforms
@MercyBCarruthers.
On Twitter @MercyBCarruther

www.MercyBCarruthers.com

For one will love *Superman* until the world blows. Some things you can't get around, under, or over. In distance or near, your heart there and his heart here *—reading this endnote.*

MERCY B CARRUTHERS

Let's Connect

Social Media

You can find me on all social platforms
@MercyBCarruthers.
On Twitter @MercyBCarruther

www.MercyBCarruthers.com

CPSIA information can be obtained
at www.ICGtesting.com
Printed in the USA
LVOW10s1146300717
543153LV00010B/254/P

9 781544 713427